SIT & SOLVE®
GREEN THUMB HANGMAN

JACK KETCH

**PUZZLE
WRIGHT
PRESS**

New York

PUZZLE
WRIGHT
PRESS
New York

An Imprint of Sterling Publishing Co., Inc.
1166 Avenue of the Americas
New York, NY 10036

ISBN 978-1-4549-2693-1

Distributed in Canada by Sterling Publishing Co., Inc.
c/o Canadian Manda Group, 664 Annette Street
Toronto, Ontario M6S 2C8, Canada
Distributed in the United Kingdom by GMC Distribution Services
Castle Place, 166 High Street, Lewes, East Sussex BN7 1XU, England
Distributed in Australia by NewSouth Books
45 Beach Street, Coogee, NSW 2034, Australia

For information about custom editions, special sales, and premium
and corporate purchases, please contact Sterling Special Sales
at 800-805-5489 or specialsales@sterlingpublishing.com.

Manufactured in China

2   4   6   8   10   9   7   5   3   1

sterlingpublishing.com
puzzlewright.com

Cover design: Gina Bonanno
Cover images from Shutterstock.com: Butterfly Hunter (butterflies);
Peter Hermes Furian (flowers); Wstockstudio (dirt)
Front cover type style: http://www.graphicsfuel.com/

RULES

Greetings, brave soul. By opening this book you have chosen to play a deadly game: hangman. Your objective is to reveal a word or phrase related to gardening or farming by correctly guessing the missing letters before you (represented by the stick figure in the gallows) are hanged. First, pick a letter and scratch off the silver circle beneath it. If that letter is correct, one or more numbers will tell you which blanks contain that letter. If you guess incorrectly, a bold ✖ will be revealed, which means you must draw in one of the stick figure's body parts. (You may solemnly strike a gong when this happens for the full effect.)

The stick figure's body has six parts: a head, a torso, two arms, and two legs. If you spell the entire word or phrase before the stick figure is completed, you survive to challenge the noose again. If you fail, it was nice knowing you. Now, if your affairs are in order, you may begin.

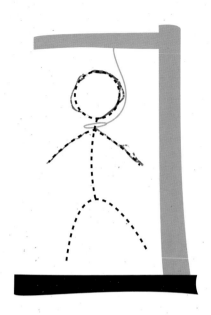

A	B	C	D	E	F	G
12				2, 15		✖

H	I	J	K	L	M
1	3		✖	5	8; 11

N	O	P	Q	R	S	T
	6, 7, 10, 14		✖	4	16	9, 13

U	V	W	X	Y	Z

H e i r l o o m
1 2 3 4 5 6 7 8

T o m a t o e s
9 10 11 12 13 14 15 16

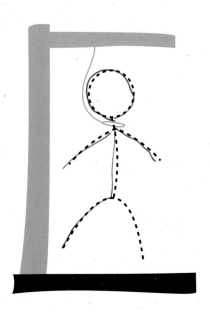

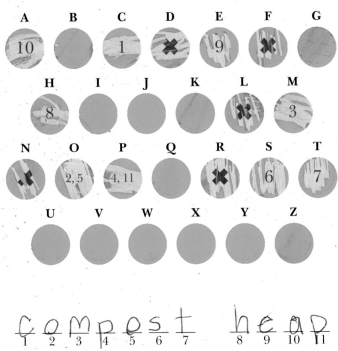

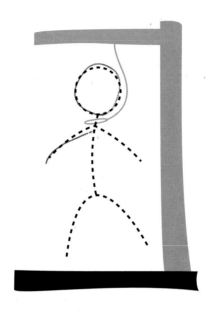

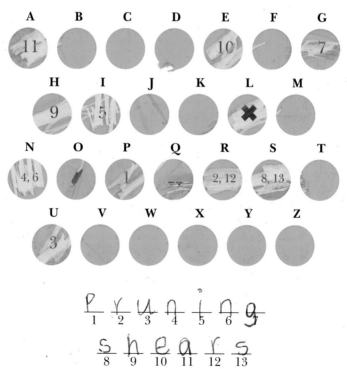

A	B	C	D	E	F	G
11				10		7

H	I	J	K	L	M
9	5			✖	

N	O	P	Q	R	S	T
4, 6		1		2, 12	8, 13	

U	V	W	X	Y	Z
3					

P r u n i n g
1 2 3 4 5 6 7

s h e a r s
8 9 10 11 12 13

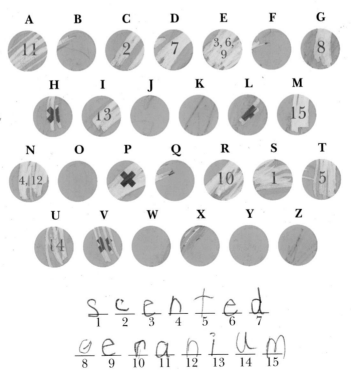

I lost

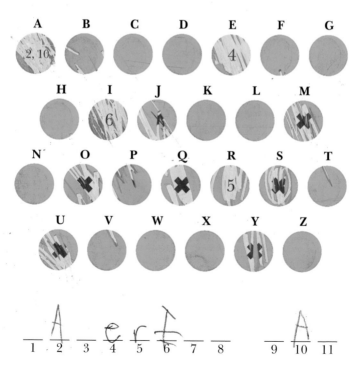

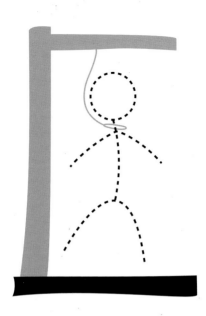

A	B	C	D	E	F	G
8				5		

H	I	J	K	L	M

N	O	P	Q	R	S	T

U	V	W	X	Y	Z

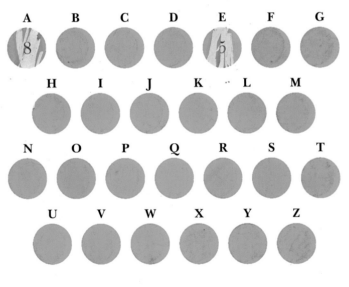

$$\overline{}_1 \quad \overline{}_2 \quad \overline{}_3 \quad \overline{}_4 \quad \overline{}_5 \quad \overline{}_6 \quad \overline{}_7 \quad \overline{}_8 \quad \overline{}_9 \quad \overline{}_{10}$$

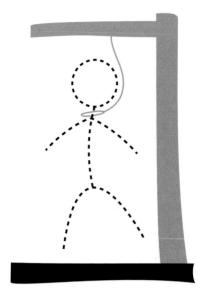

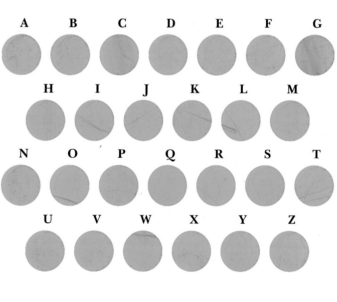

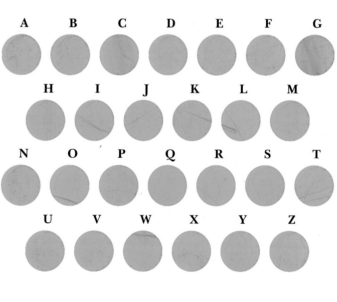

A   B   C   D   E   F   G

H   I   J   K   L   M

N   O   P   Q   R   S   T

U   V   W   X   Y   Z

$\overline{}$ $\overline{}$ $\overline{}$ $\overline{}$ $\overline{}$ $\overline{}$ $\overline{}$ $\overline{}$
 1   2   3   4   5   6   7   8

$\overline{}$ $\overline{}$ $\overline{}$ $\overline{}$ $\overline{}$
 9   10   11   12   13

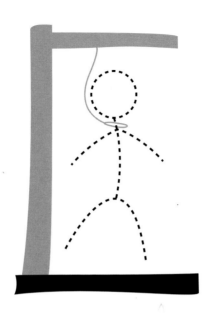

A	B	C	D	E	F	G
9				2, 4, 14		

H	I	J	K	L	M
			V		

N	O	P	Q	R	S	T

U	V	W	X	Y	Z

$$\overline{}_1 \ \overline{E}_2 \ \overline{}_3 \ \overline{E}_4 \ \overline{}_5 \ \overline{}_6 \ \overline{}_7 \ \overline{}_8 \ \overline{A}_9 \ \overline{}_{10}$$

$$\overline{}_{11} \ \overline{}_{12} \ \overline{}_{13} \ \overline{E}_{14} \ \overline{}_{15} \ \overline{}_{16}$$

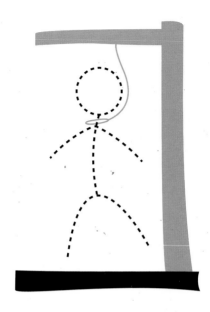

A   B   C   D   E   F   G

H   I   J   K   L   M

N   O   P   Q   R   S   T

U   V   W   X   Y   Z

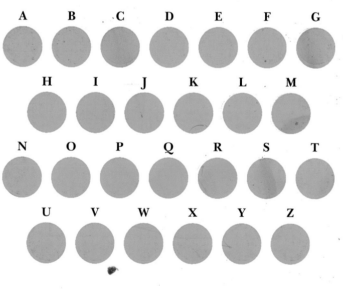

$\overline{}\ \overline{}\ \overline{}\ \overline{}\ \overline{}\ \overline{}\ \overline{}$
1 2 3 4 5 6 7

$\overline{}\ \overline{}\ \overline{}\ \overline{}\ \overline{}\ \overline{}$
8 9 10 11 12 13

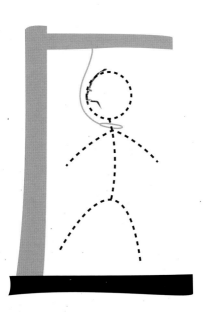

A B C D E F G

H I J K L M

N O P Q R S T

U V W X Y Z

$$\frac{}{1} \quad \frac{}{2} \quad \frac{e}{3} \quad \frac{}{4} \quad \frac{}{5} \quad \frac{}{6}$$

$$\frac{}{7} \quad \frac{}{8} \quad \frac{}{9} \quad \frac{}{10} \quad \frac{}{11} \quad \frac{}{12} \quad \frac{}{13}$$

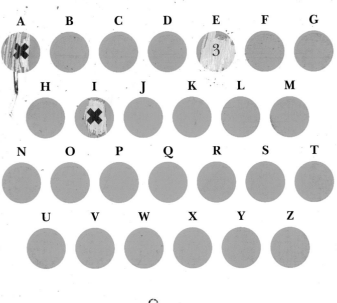

13

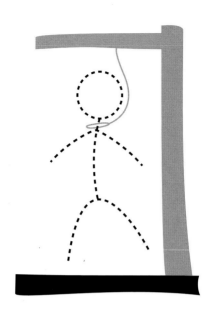

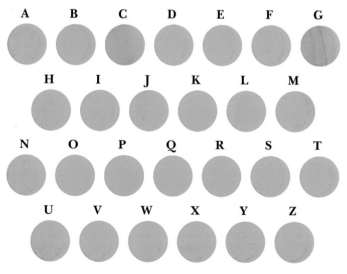

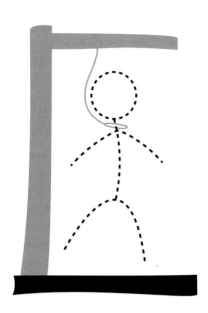

A   B   C   D   E   F   G

H   I   J   K   L   M

N   O   P   Q   R   S   T

U   V   W   X   Y   Z

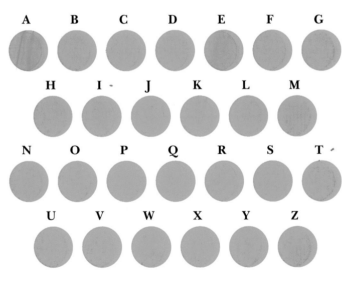

$\overline{}$ $\overline{}$ $\overline{}$ $\overline{}$ $\overline{}$ $\overline{}$ $\overline{}$ $\overline{}$ $\overline{}$ $\overline{}$ $\overline{}$ $\overline{}$
1   2   3   4   5   6   7   8   9   10 11 12

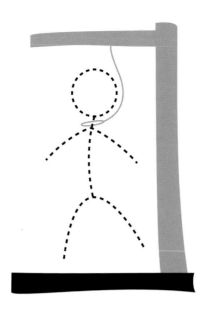

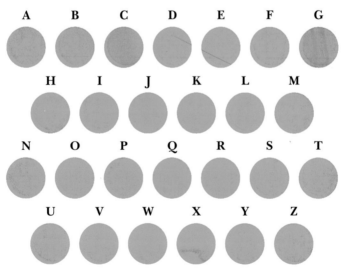

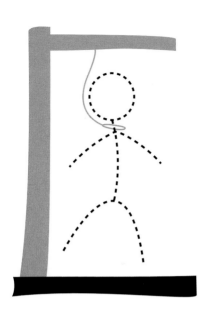

A   B   C   D   E   F   G

H   I   J   K   L   M

N   O   P   Q   R   S   T

U   V   W   X   Y   Z

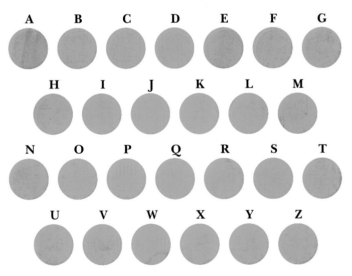

—— —— —— —— —— —— —— ——   —— —— —— ——
1   2   3   4   5   6   7   8   9   10   11   12

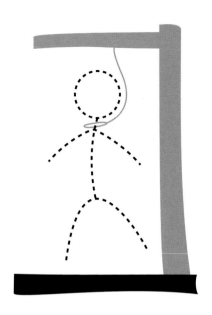

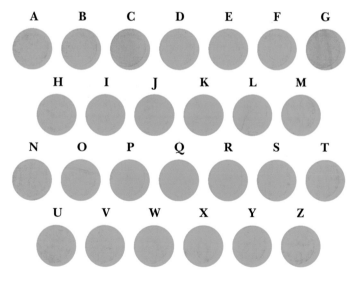

A	B	C	D	E	F	G

H	I	J	K	L	M

N	O	P	Q	R	S	T

U	V	W	X	Y	Z

$$\overline{}\ \overline{}\ \overline{}\ \overline{}\ \overline{}\ \overline{}\ \overline{}\ \overline{}\ \overline{}$$
1 2 3 4 5 6 7 8 9

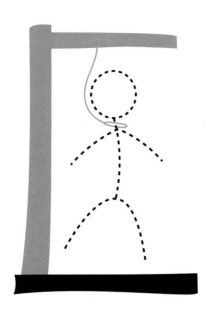

A B C D E F G

H I J K L M

N O P Q R S T

U V W X Y Z

$$-$$
$$\overline{}_1 \ \overline{}_2 \ \overline{}_3 \ \overline{}_4 \ \overline{}_5 \quad \overline{}_6 \ \overline{}_7 \ \overline{}_8 \ \overline{}_9$$

$$\overline{}_{10} \ \overline{}_{11} \ \overline{}_{12} \ \overline{}_{13} \ \overline{}_{14}$$

19

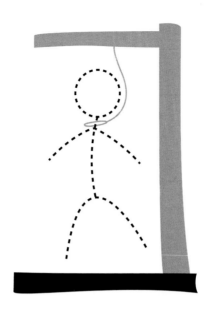

A B C D E F G

H I J K L M

N O P Q R S T

U V W X Y Z

$\overline{}$ $\overline{}$ $\overline{}$ $\overline{}$ $\overline{}$
 1   2   3   4   5

$\overline{}$ $\overline{}$ $\overline{}$ $\overline{}$ $\overline{}$ $\overline{}$ $\overline{}$ $\overline{}$
6 7 8 9 10 11 12 13

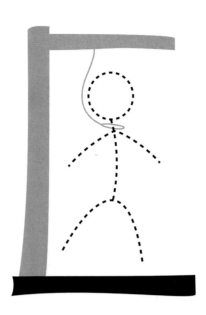

A   B   C   D   E   F   G

H   I   J   K   L   M

N   O   P   Q   R   S   T

U   V   W   X   Y   Z

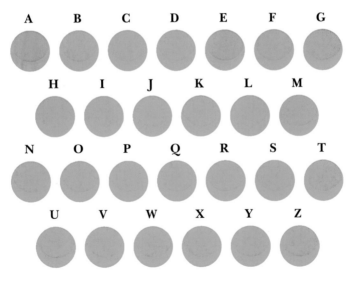

$\overline{}_{1}$ $\overline{}_{2}$ $\overline{}_{3}$ $\overline{}_{4}$ $\overline{}_{5}$ $\overline{}_{6}$ $\overline{}_{7}$ $\overline{}_{8}$

21

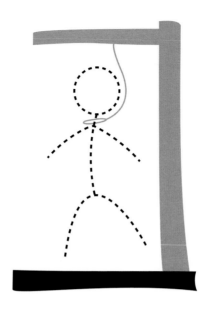

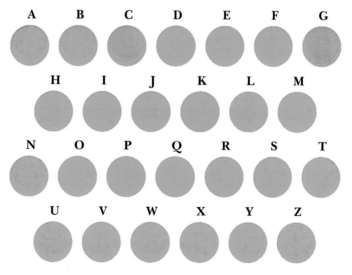

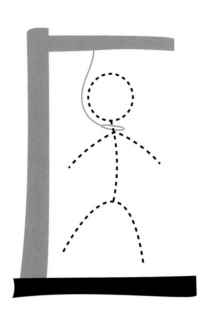

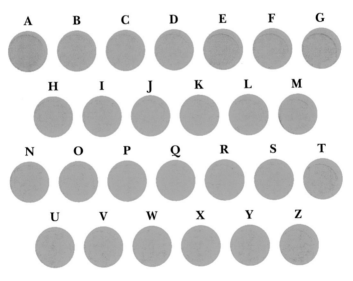

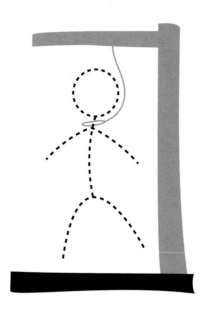

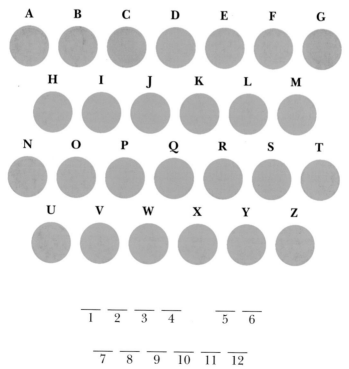

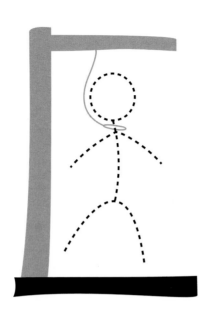

A B C D E F G

H I J K L M

N O P Q R S T

U V W X Y Z

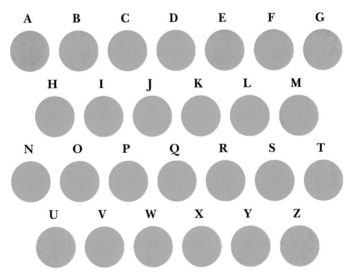

$\overline{}$ $\overline{}$ $\overline{}$ $\overline{}$ $\overline{}$ $\overline{}$ $\overline{}$ $\overline{}$ $\overline{}$ $\overline{}$ $\overline{}$ $\overline{}$ $\overline{}$
1 2 3 4 5 6 7 8 9 10 11 12 13

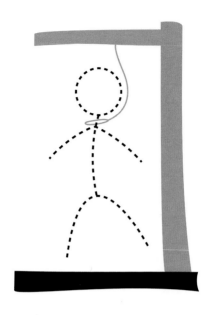

A B C D E F G

H I J K L M

N O P Q R S T

U V W X Y Z

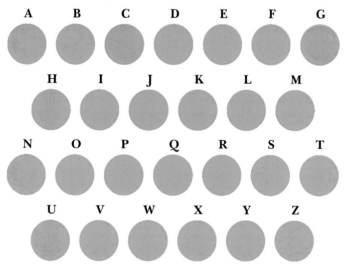

$\overline{\hspace{1em}}$ $\overline{\hspace{1em}}$ $\overline{\hspace{1em}}$ $\overline{\hspace{1em}}$ $\overline{\hspace{1em}}$ $\overline{\hspace{1em}}$ $\overline{\hspace{1em}}$ $\overline{\hspace{1em}}$
1   2   3   4   5   6   7   8

$\overline{\hspace{1em}}$ $\overline{\hspace{1em}}$ $\overline{\hspace{1em}}$ $\overline{\hspace{1em}}$ $\overline{\hspace{1em}}$ $\overline{\hspace{1em}}$ $\overline{\hspace{1em}}$
9   10   11   12   13   14   15

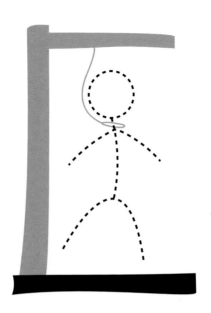

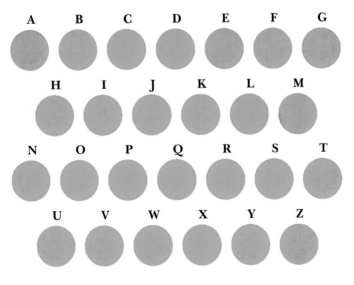

$\overline{}_1\ \overline{}_2\ \overline{}_3\ \overline{}_4 \quad \overline{}_5\ \overline{}_6\ \overline{}_7\ \overline{}_8\ \overline{}_9$

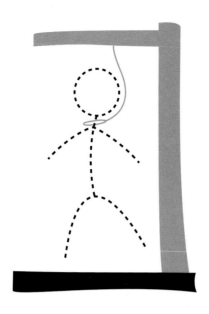

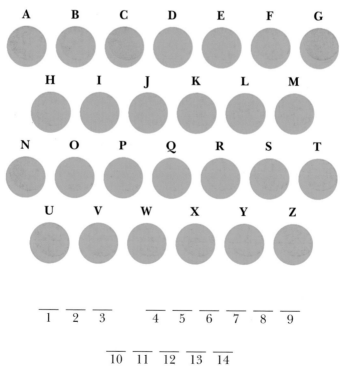

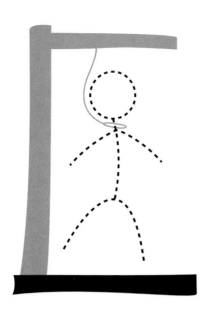

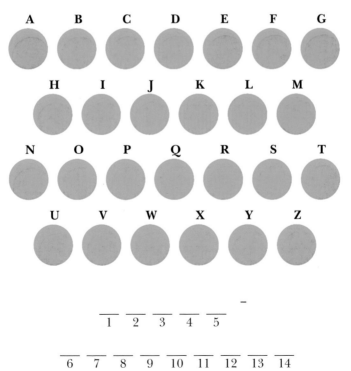

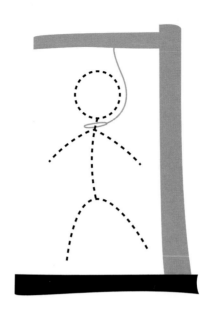

A B C D E F G

H I J K L M

N O P Q R S T

U V W X Y Z

―― ―― ―― ―― ―― ―― ―― ―― ―― ――
1　2　3　4　5　6　7　8　9　10

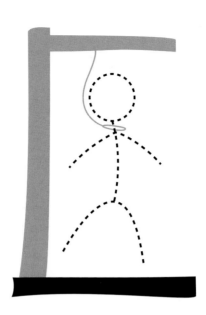

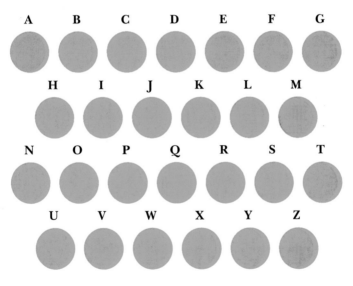

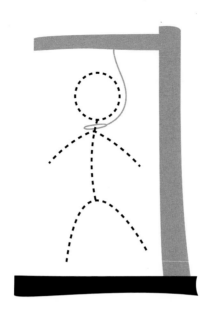

A　B　C　D　E　F　G

H　I　J　K　L　M

N　O　P　Q　R　S　T

U　V　W　X　Y　Z

$\overline{}_1$ $\overline{}_2$ $\overline{}_3$ $\overline{}_4$　$\overline{}_5$ $\overline{}_6$ $\overline{}_7$ $\overline{}_8$ $\overline{}_9$ $\overline{}_{10}$ $\overline{}_{11}$ $\overline{}_{12}$

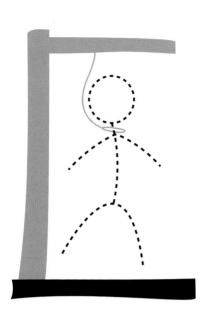

A B C D E F G

H I J K L M

N O P Q R S T

U V W X Y Z

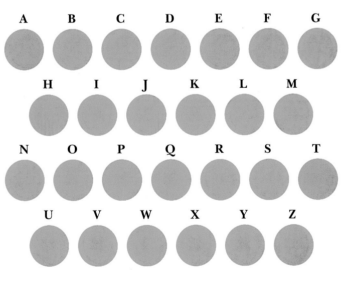

$\overline{}_1$ $\overline{}_2$ $\overline{}_3$ $\overline{}_4$ $\overline{}_5$ $\overline{}_6$ $\overline{}_7$ $\overline{}_8$ $\overline{}_9$ $\overline{}_{10}$

33

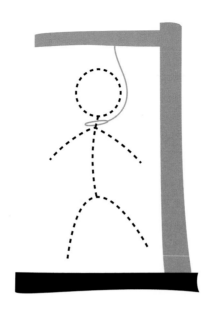

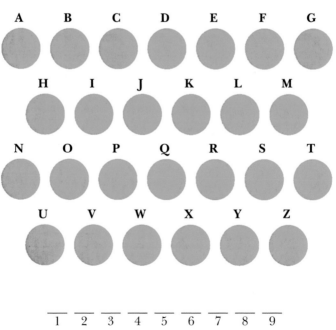

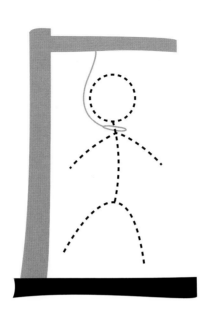

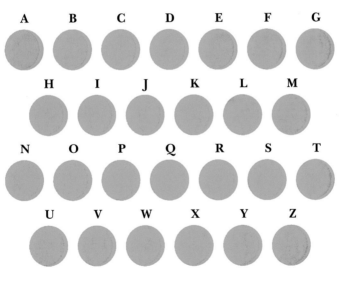

$\overline{}_{1}$ $\overline{}_{2}$ $\overline{}_{3}$ $\overline{}_{4}$　$\overline{}_{5}$ $\overline{}_{6}$ $\overline{}_{7}$ $\overline{}_{8}$ $\overline{}_{9}$

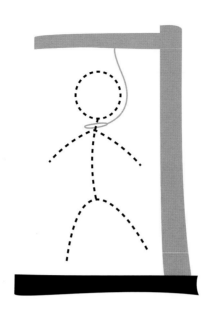

A B C D E F G

H I J K L M

N O P Q R S T

U V W X Y Z

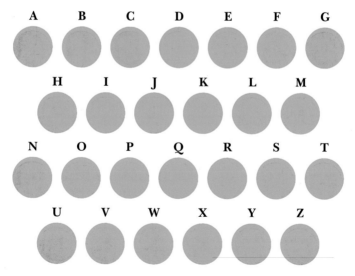

$\overline{}\;\overline{}\;\overline{}\;\overline{}\;\overline{}$, $-$ $\overline{}\;\overline{}\;\overline{}\;\overline{}\;\overline{}\;\overline{}\;\overline{}$
1   2   3   4   5   6   7   8   9   10   11   12

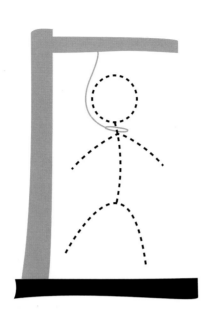

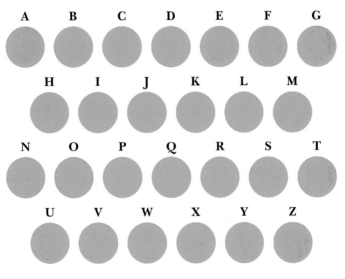

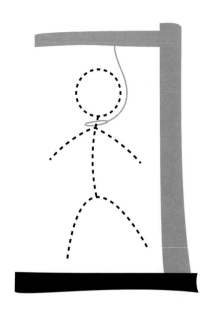

A   B   C   D   E   F   G

H   I   J   K   L   M

N   O   P   Q   R   S   T

U   V   W   X   Y   Z

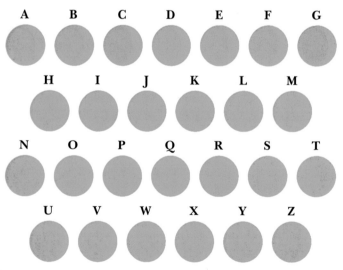

1   2   3   4   5   6   7   8   9   10

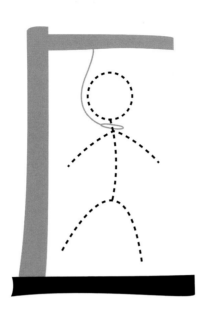

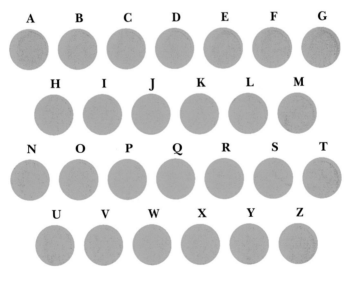

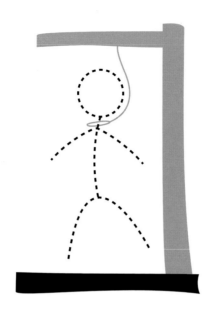

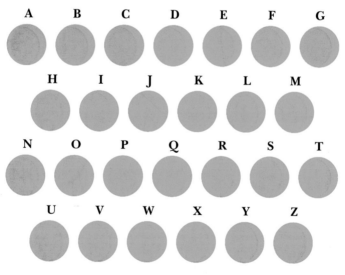

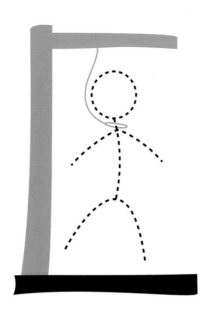

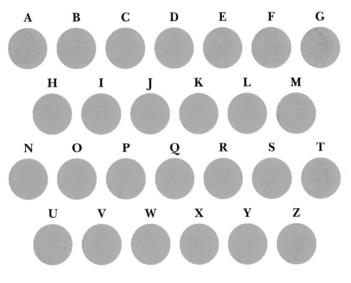

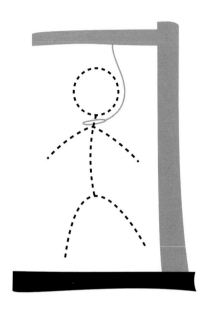

A B C D E F G
H I J K L M
N O P Q R S T
U V W X Y Z

$\overline{}$ $\overline{}$ $\overline{}$ $\overline{}$ $\overline{}$ $\overline{}$ $\overline{}$ $\overline{}$ $\overline{}$ $\overline{}$ $\overline{}$
1 2 3 4 5 6 7 8 9 10 11

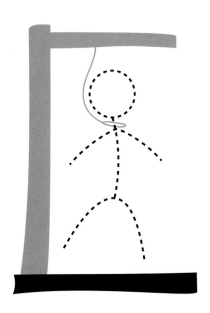

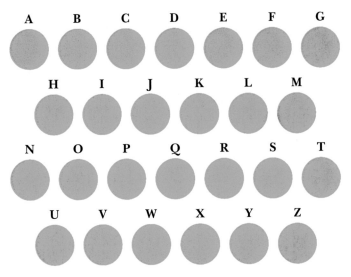

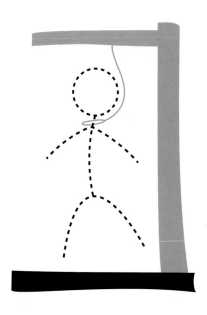

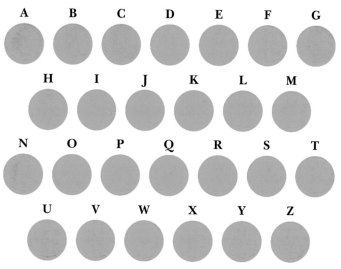

$\overline{}$ $\overline{}$ $\overline{}$ $\overline{}$ $\overline{}$ $\overline{}$ $\quad$ $\overline{}$ $\overline{}$ $\overline{}$ $\overline{}$ $\overline{}$

1 2 3 4 5 6   7 8 9 10 11

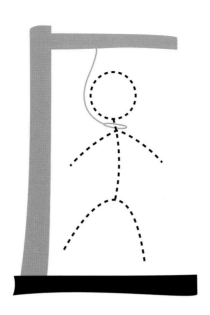

A B C D E F G

H I J K L M

N O P Q R S T

U V W X Y Z

$\overline{}_1$ $\overline{}_2$ $\overline{}_3$ $\overline{}_4$ $\overline{}_5$ $\overline{}_6$ $\overline{}_7$ $\overline{}_8$ $\overline{}_9$ $\overline{}_{10}$ $\overline{}_{11}$

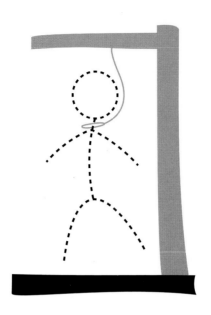

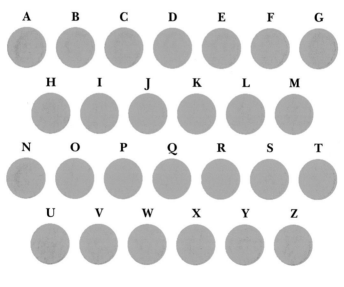

$\overline{}$ $\overline{}$ $\overline{}$ $\overline{}$ $\overline{}$ $\overline{}$ $\overline{}$ $\overline{}$ $\overline{}$ $\overline{}$ $\overline{}$

1 2 3 4 5 6 7   8 9 10 11

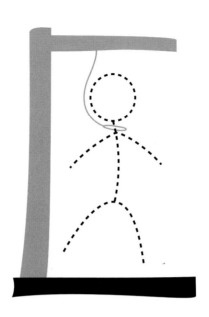

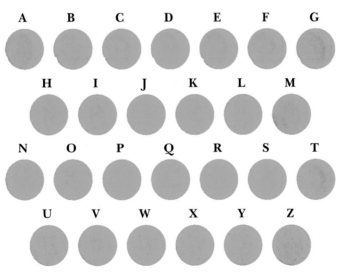

A B C D E F G

H I J K L M

N O P Q R S T

U V W X Y Z

$\overline{}$ $\overline{}$ $\overline{}$ $\overline{}$ $\overline{}$ $\overline{}$ $\overline{}$ $\overline{}$ $\overline{}$ $\overline{}$ $\overline{}$ $\overline{}$
 1   2   3   4   5   6   7   8   9   10 11 12

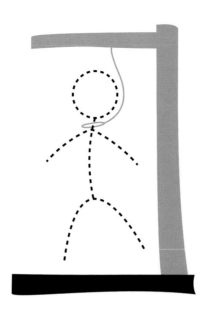

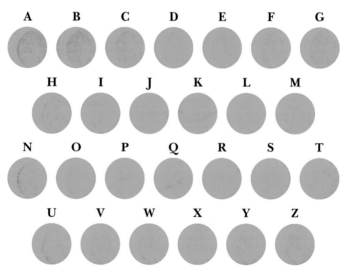

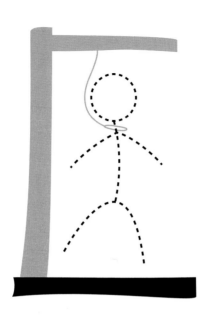

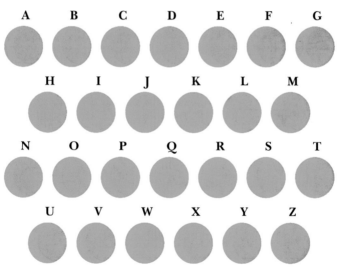

$\overline{}$ $\overline{}$ $\overline{}$ $\overline{}$ $\quad$ $\overline{}$ $\overline{}$ $\overline{}$ $\overline{}$ $\overline{}$ $\overline{}$
1 2 3 4   5 6 7 8 9 10

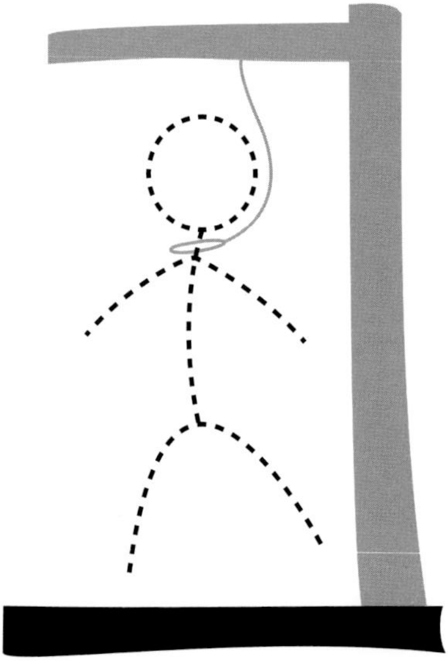

A B C D E F G

H I J K L M

N O P Q R S T

U V W X Y Z

___ ___ ___ ___ ___ ___   ___ ___ ___ ___ ___

1 2 3 4 5 6   7 8 9 10 11

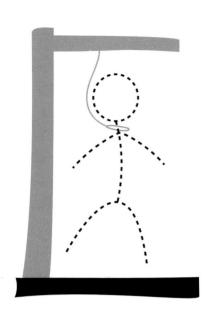

A   B   C   D   E   F   G

H   I   J   K   L   M

N   O   P   Q   R   S   T

U   V   W   X   Y   Z

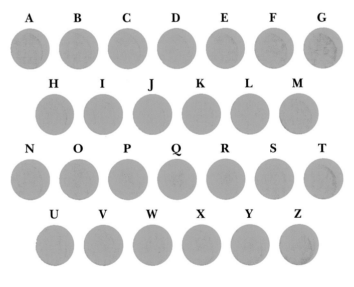

$\overline{\quad}$ $\overline{\quad}$ $\overline{\quad}$ $\overline{\quad}$ $\overline{\quad}$ $\overline{\quad}$ $\overline{\quad}$ $\overline{\quad}$ $\overline{\quad}$ $\overline{\quad}$ $\overline{\quad}$
1 2 3 4   5 6 7 8 9 10 11

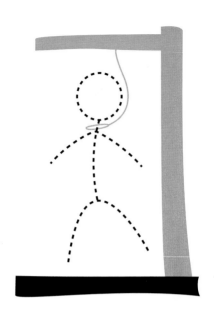

A   B   C   D   E   F   G

H   I   J   K   L   M

N   O   P   Q   R   S   T

U   V   W   X   Y   Z

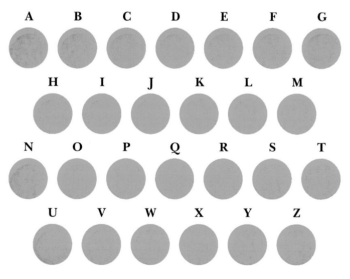

$\overline{}\ \overline{}\ \overline{}\ \overline{}\ \overline{}\ \overline{}\ \overline{}\ \overline{}\ \overline{}$
1   2   3   4   5   6   7   8   9

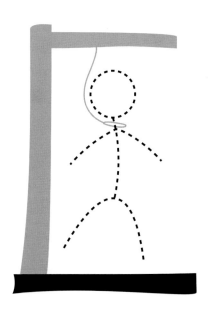

A B C D E F G
H I J K L M
N O P Q R S T
U V W X Y Z

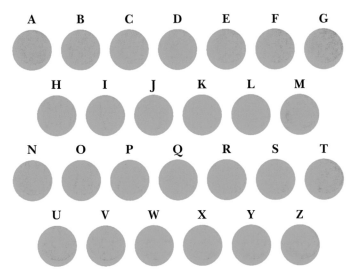

$\overline{}$ $\overline{}$ $\overline{}$ $\overline{}$　$\overline{}$ $\overline{}$ $\overline{}$ $\overline{}$ $\overline{}$ $\overline{}$ $\overline{}$ $\overline{}$
1　2　3　4　　5　6　7　8　9　10　11　12

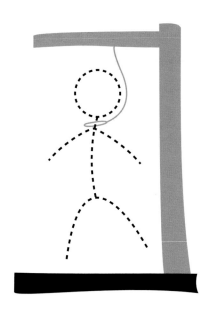

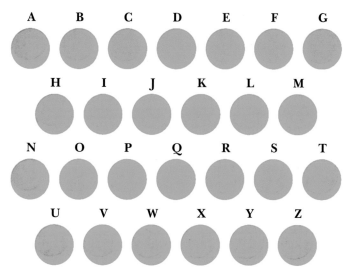

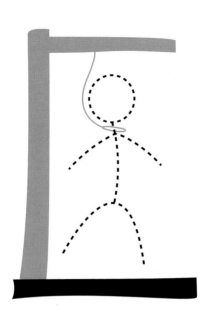

A B C D E F G

H I J K L M

N O P Q R S T

U V W X Y Z

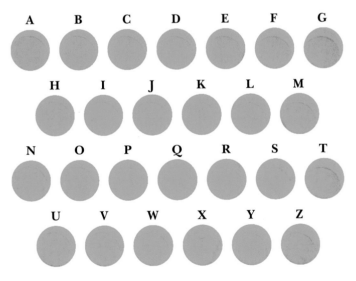

‾‾ ‾‾ ‾‾ ‾‾ ‾‾ ‾‾ ‾‾ ‾‾
1   2   3   4   5   6   7   8

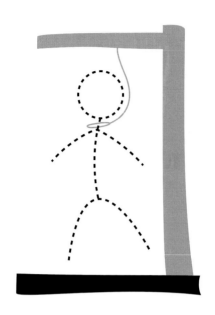

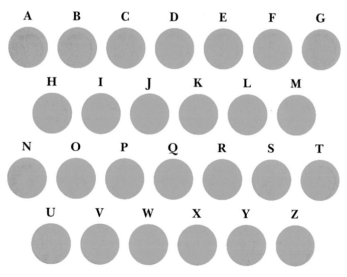

$\overline{}$ $\overline{}$ $\overline{}$ $\overline{}$ $\overline{}$ $\overline{}$ $\overline{}$ $\overline{}$ $\overline{}$ $\overline{}$ $\overline{}$
1 2 3 4 5 6 7 8 9 10 11

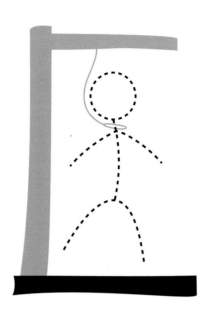

A B C D E F G

H I J K L M

N O P Q R S T

U V W X Y Z

$\overline{}$ $\overline{}$ $\overline{}$ $\overline{}$ $\overline{}$ $\overline{}$ $\overline{}$ $\overline{}$ $\overline{}$ $\overline{}$ $\overline{}$ $\overline{}$

1 2 3 4 5   6 7 8 9 10 11 12

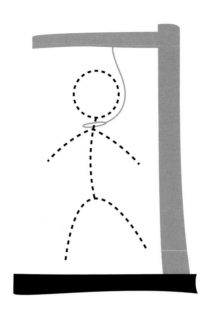

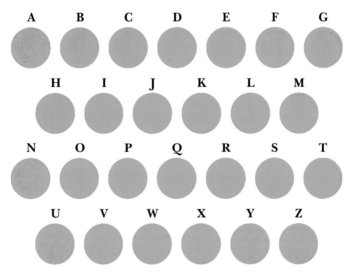

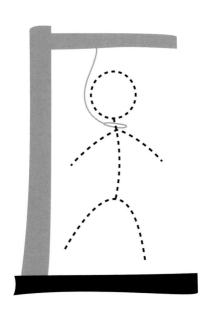

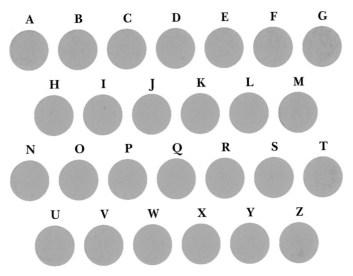

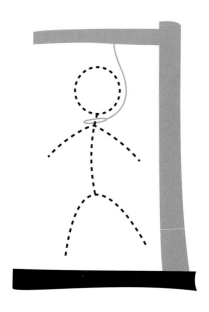

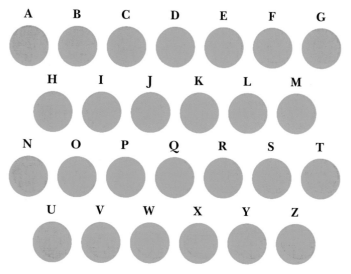

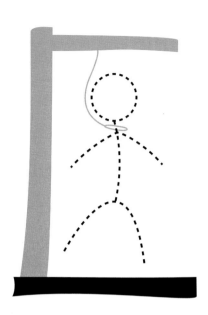

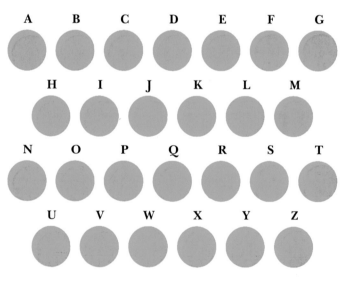

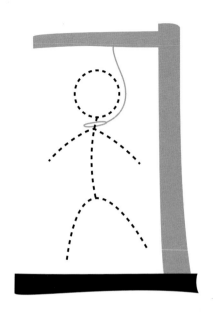

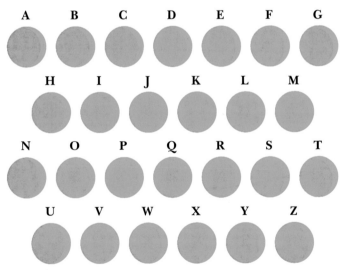

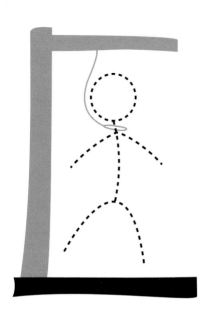

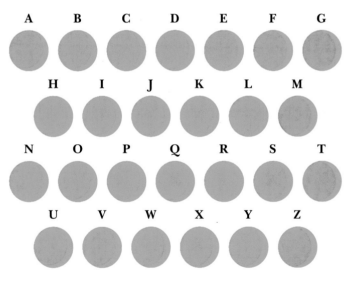

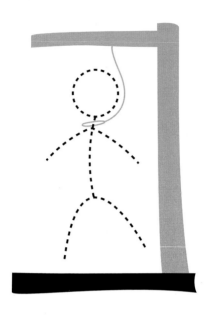

A B C D E F G

H I J K L M

N O P Q R S T

U V W X Y Z

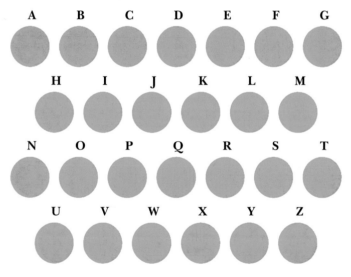

‾‾ ‾‾ ‾‾ ‾‾ ‾‾ ‾‾ ‾‾ ‾‾ ‾‾ ‾‾
1 2 3 4 5 6 7 8 9 10

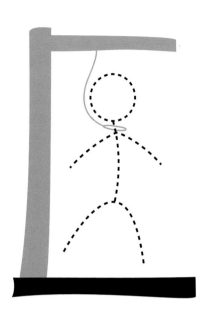

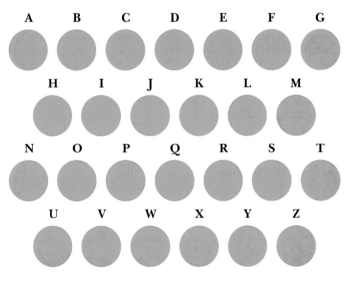

$$\overline{1} \quad \overline{2} \quad \overline{3} \quad \overline{4} \quad \overline{5} \quad \overline{6} \quad \overline{7} \quad \overline{8}$$

65

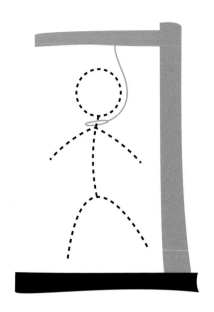

A   B   C   D   E   F   G

H   I   J   K   L   M

N   O   P   Q   R   S   T

U   V   W   X   Y   Z

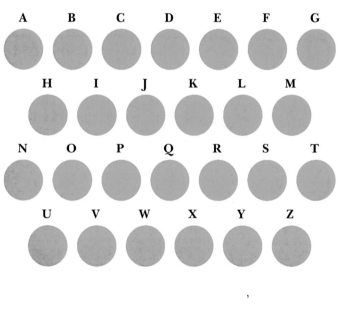

$$\overline{}_{1}\ \overline{}_{2}\ \overline{}_{3}\ \overline{}_{4}\ \overline{}_{5}\ \overline{}_{6}\ \overline{}_{7}\ \overline{}_{8}$$

$$\overline{}_{9}\ \overline{}_{10}\ \overline{}_{11}\ \overline{}_{12}\ \overline{}_{13}$$

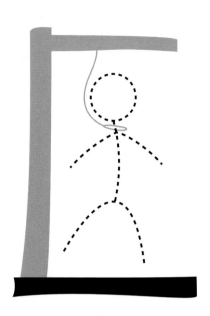

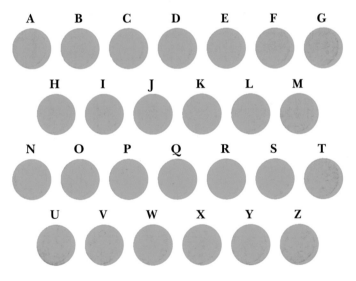

$\overline{}$ $\overline{1}$ $\overline{2}$ $\overline{3}$ $\overline{4}$ $\overline{5}$ $\overline{6}$ $\overline{7}$ $\overline{8}$ $\overline{9}$

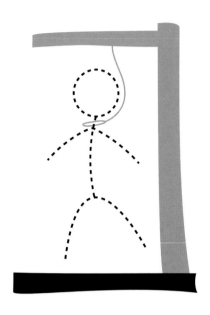

A B C D E F G

H I J K L M

N O P Q R S T

U V W X Y Z

$\overline{}$ $\overline{}$ $\overline{}$ $\overline{}$ $\overline{}$ $\overline{}$ $\overline{}$ $\overline{}$ $\qquad$ $\overline{}$ $\overline{}$ $\overline{}$
1 2 3 4 5 6 7 8 9 10 11

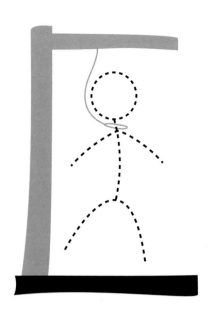

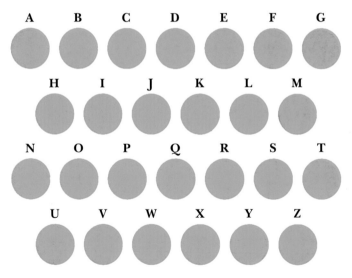

$\overline{}$ $\overline{}$ $\overline{}$ $\overline{}$ $\overline{}$ $\overline{}$ $\overline{}$ $\overline{}$ $\overline{}$ $\overline{}$ $\overline{}$ $\overline{}$

1 2 3 4 5   6 7 8 9 10 11 12

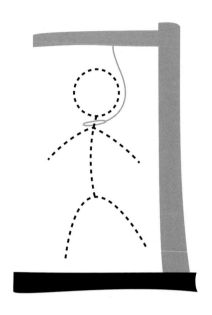

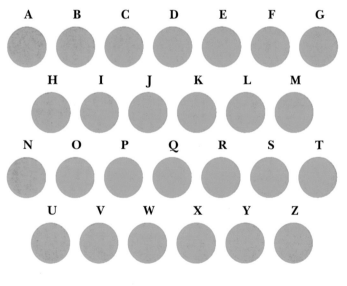

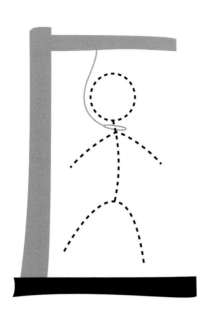

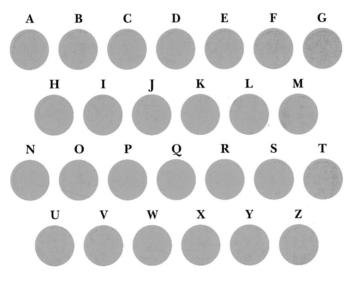

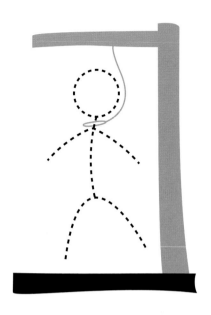

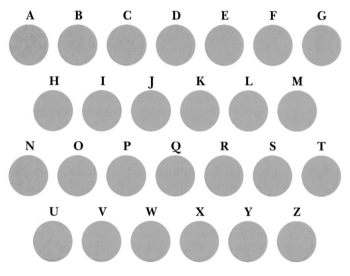

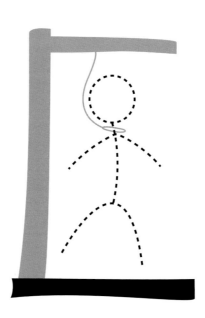

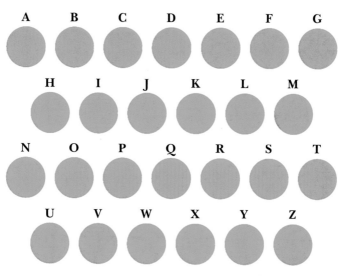

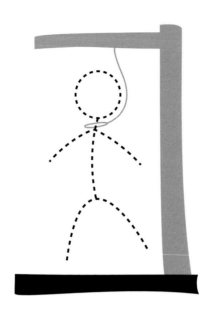

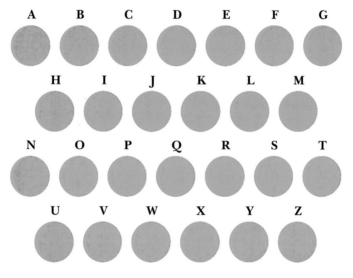

$\overline{}$ $\overline{}$ $\overline{}$ $\overline{}$ $\overline{}$ $\overline{}$ $\overline{}$ $\overline{}$ $\overline{}$
1   2   3   4   5   6   7   8   9

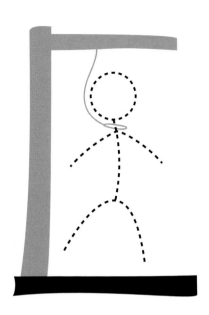

A B C D E F G

H I J K L M

N O P Q R S T

U V W X Y Z

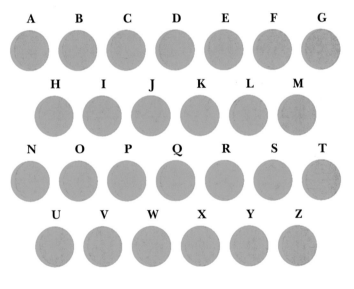

‾1‾ ‾2‾ ‾3‾ ‾4‾   ‾5‾ ‾6‾ ‾7‾ ‾8‾

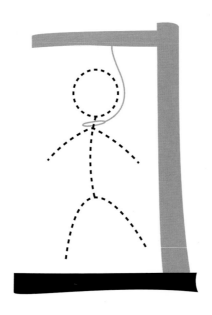

A   B   C   D   E   F   G

H   I   J   K   L   M

N   O   P   Q   R   S   T

U   V   W   X   Y   Z

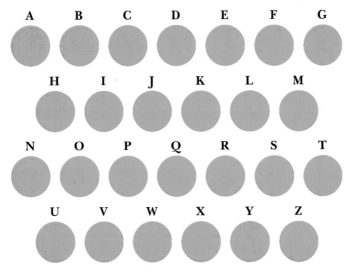

—— —— —— —— —— —— —— ——
1   2   3   4   5   6   7   8

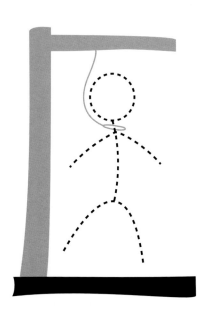

A B C D E F G

H I J K L M

N O P Q R S T

U V W X Y Z

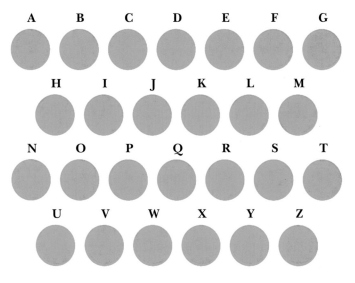

$\overline{}$ $\overline{}$ $\overline{}$ $\overline{}$ $\overline{}$ $\overline{}$ $\overline{}$ $\overline{}$ $\overline{}$
1 2 3 4 5 6 7 8 9

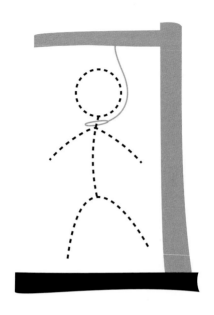

A   B   C   D   E   F   G

H   I   J   K   L   M

N   O   P   Q   R   S   T

U   V   W   X   Y   Z

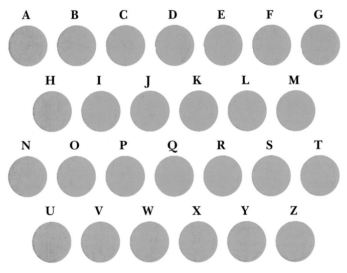

$\overline{}$ $\overline{}$ $\overline{}$ $\overline{}$ $\overline{}$ $\overline{}$ $\overline{}$ $\overline{}$ $\overline{}$ $\overline{}$ $\overline{}$ $\overline{}$
1   2   3   4   5   6   7   8   9   10   11   12

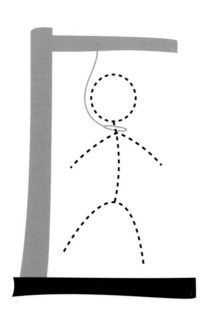

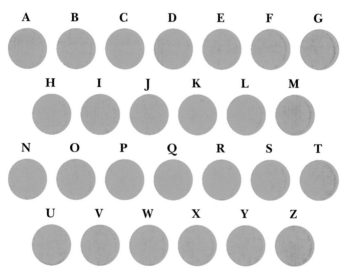

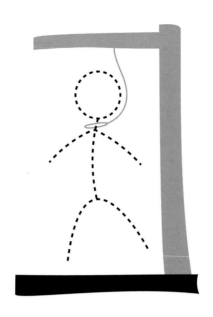

A B C D E F G

H I J K L M

N O P Q R S T

U V W X Y Z

‾1‾ ‾2‾ ‾3‾ ‾4‾ ‾5‾ ‾6‾ ‾7‾ ‾8‾

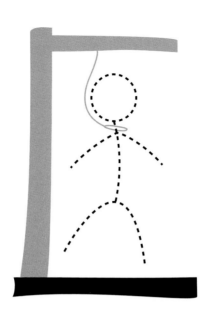

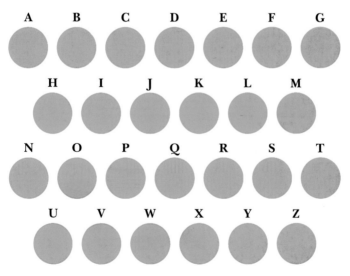

$\overline{}_1 \ \overline{}_2 \ \overline{}_3 \ \overline{}_4 \ \overline{}_5 \ \overline{}_6 \ \overline{}_7$

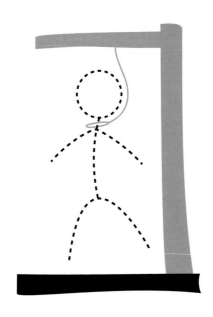

A B C D E F G

H I J K L M

N O P Q R S T

U V W X Y Z

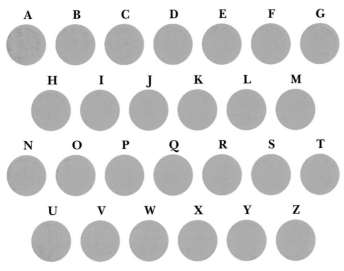

$\overline{}_1$ $\overline{}_2$ $\overline{}_3$ $\overline{}_4$ $\overline{}_5$ $\overline{}_6$ $\overline{}_7$ $\overline{}_8$

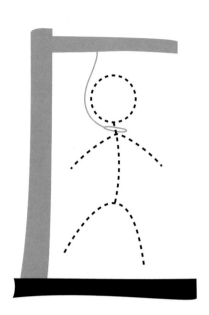

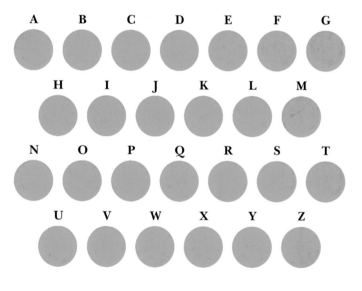

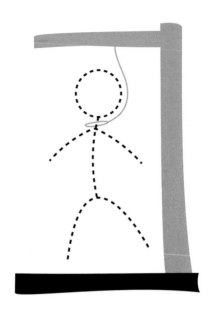

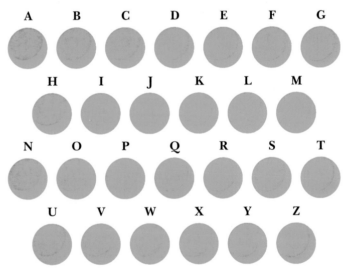

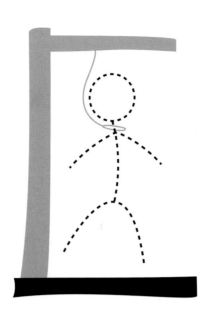

A B C D E F G

H I J K L M

N O P Q R S T

U V W X Y Z

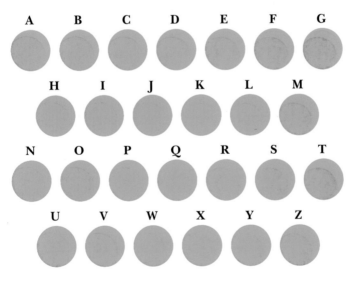

—— —— —— —— —— —— —— —— —— —— ——
1   2   3   4   5   6   7   8   9   10   11

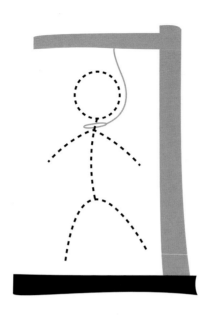

A   B   C   D   E   F   G

H   I   J   K   L   M

N   O   P   Q   R   S   T

U   V   W   X   Y   Z

$\overline{1}$ $\overline{2}$ $\overline{3}$ $\overline{4}$ $\overline{5}$ $\overline{6}$ $\overline{7}$ $\overline{8}$ $\overline{9}$

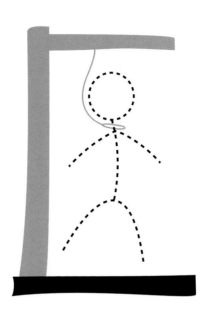

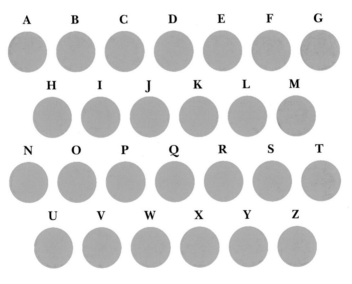

$\overline{}$ $\overline{}$ $\overline{}$ $\overline{}$ $\overline{}$ $\overline{}$ $\overline{}$ $\overline{}$ $\overline{}$ $\overline{}$ $\overline{}$
1 2 3 4   5 6 7 8 9 10 11

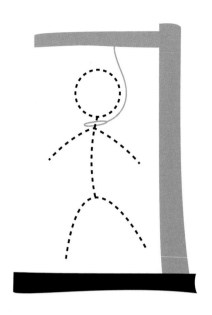

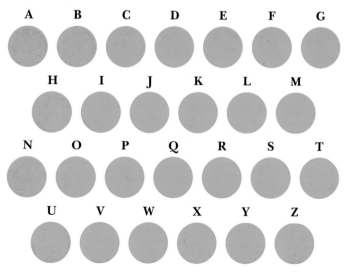

$\overline{}_{1}\ \overline{}_{2}\ \overline{}_{3}\ \overline{}_{4}\ \overline{}_{5}\qquad\overline{}_{6}\ \overline{}_{7}\ \overline{}_{8}\ \overline{}_{9}\ \overline{}_{10}\ \overline{}_{11}\ \overline{}_{12}$

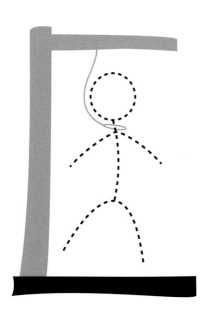

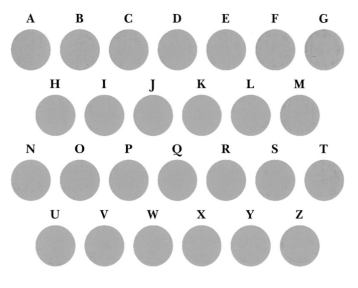

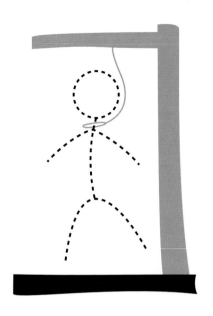

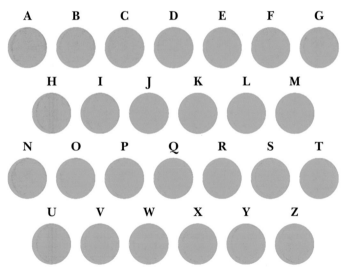

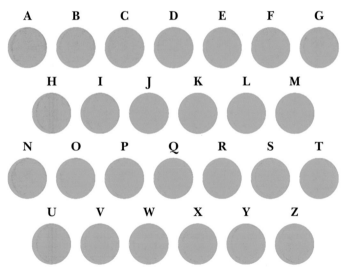

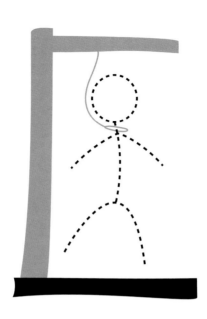

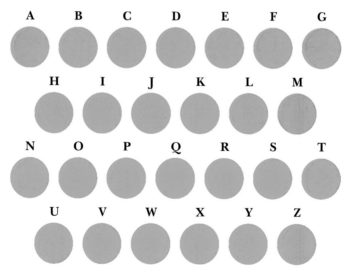

$$\overline{} \quad \overline{} \quad \overline{} \quad \overline{} \quad \overline{} \quad \overline{} \quad \overline{} \quad \overline{} \quad \overline{}$$
1   2   3   4   5   6   7   8   9

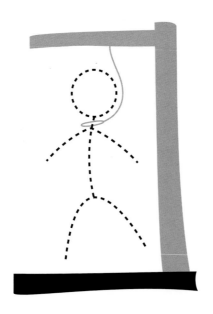

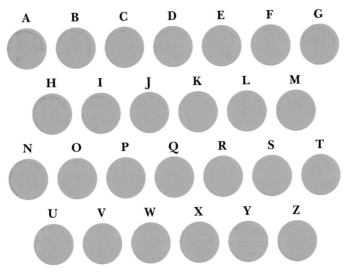

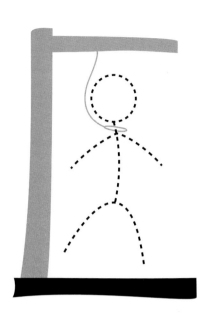

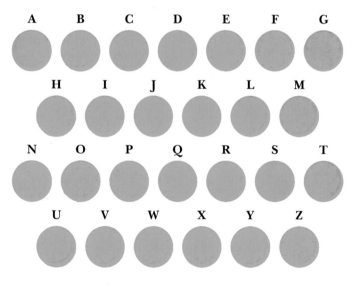

$\overline{}$ $\overline{}$ $\overline{}$ $\overline{}$ $\overline{}$ $\overline{}$ $\overline{}$ $\overline{}$
1   2   3   4   5   6   7   8

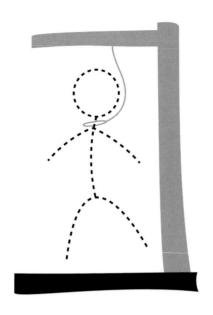

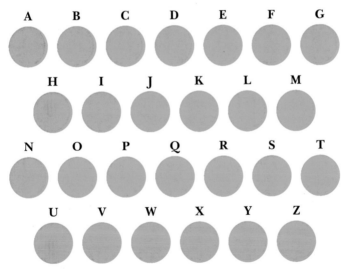

$$\overline{}\ \overline{}\ \overline{}\ \overline{}\ \overline{}\ \overline{}\ \overline{}\ \overline{}\ \overline{}\ \overline{}\ \overline{}$$
1 2 3 4 5 6 7 8 9 10 11

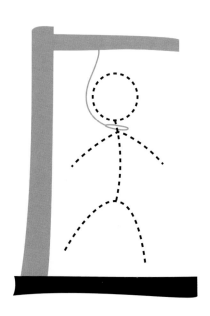

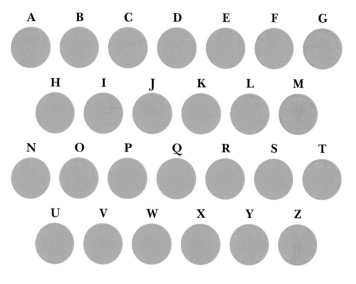

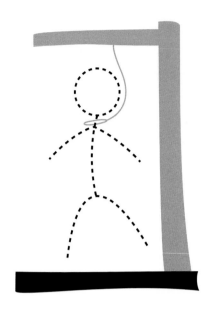

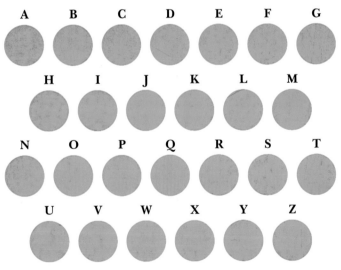

$$\overline{}\ \overline{}\ \overline{}\ \overline{}\ \overline{}\ \overline{}\ \overline{}\ \overline{}\ \overline{}\ \overline{}\ \overline{}$$

1 2 3 4 5 6 7 8 9 10 11